STAR TREK
the poems

editor
Valerie Laws

IRON
PRESS

First published 2000 by IRON Press
5 Marden Terrace
Cullercoats
North Shields
Northumberland
NE30 4PD
England
Tel/Fax (0191) 253 1901
e-mail: seaboy@freenetname.co.uk
Printed by Peterson Printers
South Shields

Book & cover design by Peter Mortimer, Michael Adam &
Valerie Laws
Set In Impact and Sand by Kitty Fitzgerald

ISBN 0 906228 77 8

IRON Press books are represented by
Signature Book Representation
Sun House
2 Little Peter Street
Manchester
M15 4PS
Tel: (0161) 834 8767
Fax: (0161) 834 8656
Email signatur@dircon.co.uk

FOREWORD

Star Trek and poetry; go together like dysentery and
zero gravity? Poetry anthologies usually have themes
that are universal, that touch all of us, like death, love,
parenthood, the seasons; it's only a matter of time
before an anthology of income tax poetry is
forthcoming. I would argue that *Star Trek* is such a
universal theme. The various series have been enter-
taining and annoying us for over thirty years. Serious
Trekkies go to conventions, dress up as characters
and carry pretend phasers and tricorders. For such
people, *Star Trek* is more of a religion, its characters
more real than real life.

But for many others too, *Star Trek* is part of the background of our lives, our childhoods. We remember
thrilling to the heroism and danger of space adventure; cutting our sexual teeth on fantasies about
Uhura's legs, Data and Spock's entrancing unattain-
ability, Picard's wonderful voice and shining head;
later mocking the clichés, cardboard sets, toupees
and corrugated heads; eventually accepting the
whole phenomenon, as we do the weather - bask in it
or hide from it, it's always there.

The opening lines of each episode, the catchphrases,
are hard-wired into our consciousness whether we
like it or not. To boldly go, beam me up Scotty, the
final frontier.....part of our common shared culture in
the same way that the myths of the Greeks and
Romans were for our ancestors. Those same myths,
which have often been recycled as *Star Trek* scripts.
When a poem of mine about *Star Trek* won a prize in

the National Poetry Competition, many people responded to it with enthusiasm, and commented that it was an unusual choice of subject. I decided that an anthology of *Star Trek* poetry would be a good idea. It turned out that there were very few such poems about, and I had to hustle for them. I discovered that many poets were secret *Trek* fans, but had never thought about writing about it. Until now.

We had submissions from all over the UK, USA, Ireland, Canada and Europe. They ranged from the heartfelt tributes of hardcore fans, to hate poems, to weird and wonderful marriages of *Star Trek* with unlikely locations and situations. How would the crew cope with the miners' strike, an encounter with a writer in residence in outer space, or a simple request for the toilet? This book holds the answer to these and many other questions.

Fundamentally, in choosing poems for this anthology, I was looking more for good poetry than sincere enthusiasm; the poems have been chosen and edited as they would have been on any subject, as I did not want this to be merely a *Trekkie* annual. However, many poets managed to combine the two. Many are well-established poets, a few are being published for the first time.

So welcome aboard; energise!

Valerie Laws
May 2000

ACKNOWLEDGEMENTS

The following poems were previously published in collections by their authors as follows:

SS Enterprise, Chelsea Reach, by Desmond Graham, in Not Falling, (seren,1999)

Lovesong to Captain JamesT Kirk, by Deryn Rees-Jones, in The Memory Tray, (seren 1994)

Ode to Scotty, by W.N. Herbert,in Cabaret McGonagall (Bloodaxe 1996)

In addition acknowledgements are due for the following poems:

Nightingale Woman, by Ruth Berman, in Masiform-D, ed. D. Langsam 1976

Hollywood Haiku, by Ruth Berman, in Film Clipper Trade Ship, ed. J & M Rondeau, 1985

The Turning of the Inland Tide, by Ruth Berman, in Rising Star, ed. K. Fleming, 1978

Sonnet from the Vulcan, by Shirley Meech, in Star Trek: The New Voyages, (Bantam 1976)

What I did in the school holidays, by Cathy Bolton, in Brando's Hat magazine.

The Star Trek Poems

TO BOLDLY GROW;
a childhood of Mr. Spock, not Dr. Spock

1

SUBHADASSI

Unpasteurized

It was in the golden age of fish fingers
acrylic came from outer space
and saved us in the suburbs
in the colour of our shag-pile carpet.
Burnt orange. I lounged on it
with half a pint of green top milk,
dipping ginger nuts and watching Star Trek.

Mum's phaser was always set to stun
till Star Date Bed Time, The Final Frontier
when she beamed me up the stairs,
tucked me in and kissed me goodnight in Klingon
leaving me to dreams of dilithium,
The Power Source,
Lieutenant Uhura's tiger eyes.

MANDY COE

Bred to boldly go

no further than Butlins, the future
was not an option for us.
Ink stained and sweaty, we slumped at desks:
11-plus failures in green nylon sweaters.
Preparing for life
by memorising Kings and Queens.

Menstrual cramps, Benny Hill,
Nimble-girls with tape-measure belts
-the distant rumble of feminism had not yet
cast doubts on our gentle mutilations:
 bleach, mascara, crippling high heels.
 So my sister and I forgave Star Trek
the tin-foil bikinis, the obligatory mushy kiss.

For here was the whisper of revolution: the promise
of a future beyond shop-work and babies. Jobs
never dreamed of: communications, engineering,
science. Single women in space. And of course
we wanted to be Spock, serene Spock, his face
bathed in the cool, blue light of computer logic.

Comrades, adventure, putting wrongs to right:
this was a ship-shape world of quantifiable tasks.
No groping in cinemas, paired in a foursome
with someone you hate,
 just to be with your best friend

No Whicker's World. No Sunday-dinner-violence
No boils. No Vietnam.

Dee dum da-da-da-da dum, sang my sister and I,
thrilled by the simplest of revolutionary ideas:

it doesn't have to be like this.

CARDINAL COX

Cabin Boy

We marched on alien soil
the Captain, Crew and me.
Out beyond Mars
between Pleiades and Polaris
between Nationwide and Panorama
the Starship journeyed on.
At seven I was a cabin-boy
invisible but with them
sharing danger after tea
and all women from
the same world as Pan's People.
Then, when eight, the final foe,
schedulers sent the ship off-course
and I made do with Terry & June.

MIKE MORGAN

Remember

I remember when I was young and callow
Kirk wrestled with the victim of the week
in quarries so mundane, in plots so shallow,
under suns that were double, always in trouble
and we hung onto the edge of our seats
hardly daring to breathe
as he acted out our schoolboy dreams
in a golden shirt with precisely torn seams
and fought his way through polystyrene rocks;
those background props that fandom mocks,
to win a last-minute victory that made us say,
' Doesn't that contradict last week, by the way? '

To be young again! Could even Mr. Spock
with Vulcan logic roll back that clock
and make it the way it used to be?
When Shatner had his own hair and we
didn't realise how poor his singing was,
when we thought we'd conquer the stars
and have space-age pills for tea.
Bring back that technicolor past
and watch out fot that Dyson sphere, Scotty!
No, I guess even heroes don't last
and all we can do to thank the cast
is remember.

CATHY BOLTON

What I did in the school holidays

Week two: I went to the moon.
My dad, a cleaner for the Starship Enterprise,
sneaked me on board. I hid in the broom cupboard:
twelve days with nothing to eat
but a tin of Spam and packets of Smash.
Soon as we touched base, I was out there.
The others took yonks, putting on suits
made from sewn-together bottle tops
and plastic bubble masks. I don't know why,
the air was deliciously fresh,
smelt of Fairy Liquid: the Americans lied.
The surface of the moon was covered in slime,
the colour of green ice-pops; slippery as soap.
I climbed a small hill, planted my signed photo
of Donny Osmond in a grove
of madonnas and stubbed candles.
The crew played five-a-side; tried to fool gravity
with a water-filled johnny. It was a no-score draw.
Coming back, Captain Kirk had a panic attack
so, I read the map while Dad drove us home.

ALAN BOAG

Of course we knew
(Strathclyde University Physics Class.1967)

We knew,
Of course we knew,
(Apart from those who just believed).
First the moon,
Next, shortly, Mars;
The stars;
Then finally,
The Enterprise.

We knew
That in these labs and lecture rooms,
Where one day Scott himself would sit,
we, or one of us,
would help to make it so.

A generation on,
Those laws, unchanged,
grow every day more/ strange,
While we, who would have changed them,
Changed ourselves.

But still,
We know,
Of course we know
(Apart from those who just believe);

First the moon, (that's done)
Next, one day, Mars;
The stars;
Then finally,
The Enterprise.

DESMOND GRAHAM

S.S. Enterprise: Chelsea Reach

My parents met on the *S.S. Enterprise.*
Mr. Spock took them to *The Servites*
where her father burst in and protested
but they married anyway.

My father worked for Capt. Kirk,
who found him most reliable and promised him
an extra stripe but grew severe at talk of wages.

During the Empire wars my mother altered uniforms,
travelling the universe on crafts of every sort
with me beside her.

When peace came back my father landed
and stretched out on Sundays
in a chair beside the anthracite.

My mother mourned so manfully
when finally he was grounded,
but survived by raiding the in-flight medicines.

Marrying the padre, she then lived in bliss
till she too finally was brought down.
leaving such love:

my father, out of the limelight,
never in the picture,
and she off-stage altogether

but doing her repairs, secretly,
with glue and oil and hairpins,
keeping us on course for the stars.

THE ENTERPRISE CULTURE;
the Warp Factor in all our lives

STEPHEN WADE

A new life-form experiences its first anxiety attack

It was beautiful before they came.
I never knew dreams and fantasies.
I could concentrate on my useful work,
Placing valves in the correct positions
Sitting by the assembly line, contented.

But THEY arrived, the whole evil gang,
And I've never known sleep since.
First there was the chubby one, dazzling
With his commands and madman's rage for order.
Then the Scot, obsessed with metal working parts,
And the poem-spouting alien with rabbit's ears.

They brought me restless thoughts,
With their talk of distant galaxies.
That imperial romance of land beyond Crewe.
I scream all night, fearful, imagining
Malfunctions due to poorly fitted valves
And I see manic faces of earthlings in free-fall.
Yes, I was clueless till THEY paid a call.

KAREN R. PORTER

the final frontier beckoning

travelling down light - year arcs
chasing frontier dreams and a need to know
and when we landed on the moon
I knew it could happen:
intergalactic magic, rubbing the stars for luck
with a warp speed rainbow trail reflecting the eyes
of marvellous beings welcoming and welcomed
without xenophobic strictures.
Here was the love of learning
and adventure never lost from childhood,
the chance to believe that we could make it so.

KEITH ALLEN DANIELS

'Television isn't heaven '

Messrs. Asimov, Heinlein and Blish
have returned through my satellite dish.
But no one can see
or hear them but me,
as they swim through the channels like fish.

With a swirl of diaphanous fins
they're atoning for various sins.
Purgation is hell.
but they're taking it well,
and they're happy when Star Trek begins.

DAVID BATEMAN

The Enterprise

Had a car I called the Enterprise
after I discovered too late
that it was warped in the factory
and the engine couldn't take it.

I tried to boldly make it
down to Cornwall where I hadn't been before
but broke down less than half way there
and paid a fortune just getting home.

Got it sort of fixed but it never
really went like it should. Always this
or that wrong with it. Finally sold it
to some sucker for half its so-called worth;

bought a replacement I called the Challenger
but that's another, altogether sadder story.

DAVID BATEMAN

To Boldly Stay
" mission: to explore strange new worlds..."

But what of those who explore
the ordinary new worlds ?
The worlds like all the other worlds
where Joe Soap went before ?

Other heroes boldly go
to strange and distant realms of space,
but what about this simple place
we all already know ?

We'd like to travel too
just like those other bold explorers
sailing beyond the sky's auroras,
but the fact is we have other things to do.

We know they must be tough,
those brave ones who trek from star to star,
but for we who'll never travel quite so far
our life on Earth seems challenge enough.

RODNEY WOOD

Muddy Waters

After an episode with Uhura
displaying her permanent earring,
short skirt, modelling the colour black,
saying : 'Hailing frequencies still open , sir'
and then fading into the background
I went to a club in Reading.
Being the wrong colour I sat at the back
while Muddy Waters flashed his rings.
No one bothered me - why should they
when we're sharing the same sounds.
And I wondered about Lokai and Bele,
people who only have hate
and time for Mr Bones.

Clunk-click, every sling-shot round the sun

Tinker, tailor, soldier, Klingon
I wandered lonely as a Cardassian
Targ,Targ, burning bright
Sweet holograms are made of this
An apple a day keeps the E..M.H. away
Mind over anti-matter
There's plenty more whales in the sea
Round the world in 80 nanoseconds
Faster than a speeding warp
All work and no play make Vulcan a dull boy
Everyone wants to rule the Federation
Can't get no latinum
Odo to a Nightingale
I found my Trill on Blueberry Hill
Loose tribbles sink ships
Somewhere over the worm-hole
Your captain wants YOU
The answer, my friend, is blowing in the Nexus
You're only supposed to blow the bloody
bulkheads off !
Swing low sweet Enterprise.

GIOVANNI MALITO

Willy

Willy's one immutable dream
is to play doctor with Bev Crusher
or, in fact, with any, at least
partially sentient, female being
extant in the universe. But, it seems
there are few who are impressed
by him or his extensive knowledge
of any and all things Star Trekkular.

Sometimes, Willy wears his official
Next Generation officer's uniform
to his classes at the Community College
where he is met with open derision.
And no matter how polished his emblem
is, or how sharp his pants are creased
the girls continually aspire to, and attain,
bold new heights in total resistance,

Yet, Willy, in true Rodenberry spirit
has not and will not give up all hope.
He fully believes, with every carbon fibre
of his being, that there is a woman
somewhere in this star system who thinks
Spock is sexy and who knows that the T
in James T. Kirk stands for Tiberius.
You see, Willy considers himself a trekker,

never to be confused with a trekkie. Trekkies,
says Willy, urgently need to get a life.

Kevin Cadwallender

Julian and the Final Frontier

Julian is a Klingon 'bird of prey' pilot.
He studies IT at the university,
he speaks several languages,
all of them are from Star Trek!

In the summer he signs on
citing as his preferred occupation;
Pilot: cloaked or uncloaked

The D.S.S. supervisor has bought
an English/Klingon Dictionary.
She is learning how to say
'suspended from benefits'
but for now she leans across
the counter and says,
'do KHA'
which means,
'That is unfortunate.'

Julian duly amends his form
to 'anything in computers'
(Borg and Cardassian empire excluded).
How far he is willing to travel
depends on the warp capacity of his 'wessell'
a clapped-out Ford Fiesta
bought via the internet from
the Ferrenghi Chemistry student
at Manchester University.

Julian got a job at McDonalds
where he is an extra, waiting
to be beamed off the planet's surface,
uses his expertise to teach the
customer service droids
the perfect Vulcan death grip.

Patrick Snape

Klingons

He was a Trekkie
And enjoyed making cosmic metaphors.
I was Picard, complex and hard,
Him, he was Jim,
Super cool under pressure, but not slim.

We, meaning you and me,
He likened to two bright shooting stars
Passing through the sky,
Destined to flare, then die.

That logical equation (not a guess)
Was predicted before
our flight paths finally separated,
Narrowly avoiding the mess
Of a fatal crash to earth.

But why the long descent,
Why were we so intent
on a self-destructive
Trajectory to oblivion?

The answer is quite logical
And elementary:
We are both Klingons,
And Klingons as we know
Find it impossible to let go !

ROSEANN PANNIER-TAYLOR

Tribute

No one knew it would last thirty years
Making an impact on television
That would last forever.
Fans flock to screenings
And converge on conventions
Dressed as Spock and Kirk
Or Worf and Data
Alienating the real world to carry on
A tradition of peace and harmony
As a new crew blasts off
Bringing a younger generation
Into the realms of space.
Who would have thought
That all of this 'nonesense' would last
over a quarter of a century
Sparking the imaginations
of three generations.

SHEENAGH PUGH

Never a Trekker

See, I could never take the optimism.
That pan-galactic Federation, run
by the good guys *(please!)*. Harmony and peace
spreading like muck; even the Klingons join

the party in the end....Where's the amusement
in a world that just keeps getting better ?
What do you do for angst, grievance, a cause ?
Now, Brit-style SF was another matter:

all shaky sets and dark dystopian dreams.
If there was going to be a Federation,
it'd be firmly in the hands of bastards.
The good guys would be outlaws on the run,

and not so good either, and they'd lose
in the end....Meanwhile, we could share
their griefs, their wounds, their failed relationships,
their pangs of guilt...God, it was fun to suffer.

Infinite Diversity: each to his own.
I know America's sunny side up
by nature, and good luck to them, I say,
but I'm a Celt: I can't handle hope.

FRIENDS, ROMULANS, CREW MEMBERS
mind melding with the cast

Scott E. Green

Geographers;
a poem in four tankas

Two outsiders man
the bridge of the Enterprise.
They are apart from the rest
of the crew. Men who
seek to define boundaries.

Data brings a vast
mind to draw a precise map
of the heart and to walk its
pathways and routes.
Becoming part of that map.

Worf brings vast strength to
find where and when he must go
beyond the boundaries of
blood and honour so
he can restore family.

Geographers whose
passions propel them to
create maps of lands as yet
undiscovered, lands they must
know, lands that are journey's end.

Debjani Chatterjee

Enterprising Harmony - a Star Trek ghazal

Science Officer, Mr Spock, raises pointed
                              hand and brow,
and in his usual fashion says: 'Live long and prosper.'

I am James T Kirk, Star Trek Captain of the Enterprise;
united, my universal crew live long and prosper.

But Mr Spock is always showing off, upstaging me.
The last thing I want is for him to live long and
                              prosper.

He's a pointy-eared Vulcan imp while I'm only human,
and drama needs conflict - so we can't live long and
                              prosper.

On the other hand, our ratings call for happy endings;
so, for better or worse, Spock and Kirk live long and
                              prosper.

Sean Russel Friend

Data

Computer, why must the good die young?
  (insufficient data)
And why do I see her face in the stars?
  (insufficient data)
Computer, has Tasha gone to Heaven?
  (insufficient data)
Or is her spirit in the ship itself?
  (insufficient data)

Computer, what is the meaning of death?
  (there are six-hundred-and -fifty-billion
  entries in that category:
  please be more specific...)

Max Scratchmann

Mr Data

Mr Data
        with your quizzical glance
        and silver skin

Next generation's
        Tin Man
if you only had a heart

Unblinking
you soar through space
in search of the Emerald City

Click your heels together,
        Data, click your heels,
There's no place like home

Deborah P. Kolodji

Sonnet from the ship (NC 1701)

I am a ship. I never sailed a sea,
as a science fiction dream that would not die.
No oceans I have crossed but imaginations's galaxy
was mine. Then television officials waved goodbye.

I was told my crew was dead. Yet I steer through the
night.
Has cancellation stilled my engines, as they thought?
Adventure has not ceased as I move towards the light
on new voyages with my starry camelot.

Now resurrected, though I was never truly dead,
a pheonix they would make of what I was.
So let them think that I'm back - I will go on as I have
done
to delight those who explore the worlds my captain
does.

To NBC, I was an empty dream that couldn't be
Yet, a space shuttle bears my name,
Smithsonian crowds gaze at me.

Deborah P. Kolodji

Amanda's Lament

My son, where have you gone?
When did you go away?
When did raised eyebrows replace a smile?
When did you cease to play?

When others teased you, I watched
knowing the human inside you cried tears.
I reached out to help, but you stood alone,
growing more Vulcan through the years.

It's been years since your last visit
since your father and you disagree.
Though loving my husband, I do miss my son -
is it illogical for you to miss me?

Shirley Meech

Sonnet from the Vulcan: Omicron Ceti Three

I thought the memory of you was gone -
I thought it buried underneath the years.
But now it rises, bright as Vulcan dawn,
And I remember you, and Earth and tears.
Your tears were falling like the rain of Earth;
You were the storms and roses of Earth's spring.
You could not know that almost from my birth,
The rites of Vulcan bound me to T'Pring.
I could not break those ties; I had no choice -
Returned to space, left you and Earth behind.
But still I heard the echo of your voice,
Found rain and wind and roses in my mind.
You told me that you loved me, and you cried.
I said I had no feelings. And I lied.

Joy H. Mann

A Logical Place To Raise The Young

We left our world
you and I
for flesh on which
to raise our young,
for long, ripe spines
in which to lay my eggs.

We left for skin and bone
and blood to help
them grow.

But

this is no human spine, my One.
This is no 'man'.

His thoughts are driving me insane,
his blood runs cold and green.

Joy H. Mann

The Companion's Veil

Oh, Love...will you know me when you gaze
into her eyes; will
you remember how I cared for you?
When your hand touches hers,
will her body,
her flesh,
each cell close off this love
I feel? Zephran,
was I nothing to you
but a scintillating light,
could you not feel my love in each
immortal cell?

This is as close, as close
as we can ever be: you
touching her, me
forever reaching out, trapped
within the veil
of her skin.

G.O. Clark

Captain Kirk in retirement

It's sad to see this
once proud captain of the
starship Enterprise doing one-liners
and car commercials,

no longer going 'where
no man has gone before,' but then
again, the galaxy can be a very cold and
lonely place, so his preference

for the warm fuzzy feeling
of a human smile, and the known
space of the interstate highway system,
does follow a certain logic.

Lindsay Kelly

Klingon Battle Prayer

If I am to live this day
Grant that I live well.
Do not let my weapons fail me
As I despatch my enemies
Upon the road to hell.

But if I am to die this day
Grant that I die well.
Do not let my courage fail me
As the killing blow descends
And my comrades howl the knell.

For if I should survive this day
There will be another.
As sure as darkness follows light
And carrion birds the battle,
Glory will call me to the fight;
And sooner, later, who can say,
My spirit will arrow to the heroes' heaven.
Will it be tomorrow or today?

Today is a good day to die.

Jackie Curry

(War) Arc

The stench and noise of war
Are lost in space.
The flash and bang of battle
Become slow soundless pyrotechnic
Bright lazy blossoming into
The cold, hard inky vacuum.
Phaser fire
Obscene graffiti between the stars.

We see this through a window
View screen dividing one reality
From another,
Two universes parted by
A micron's width;
Hot hell's contrast on this side.
Smoke filled space
With zinging smell of frazzled circuits
And meatiness of frying flesh.
Cries of command and anguish
Clamouring in the acrid air.

Hard to remember that
On the other side
Behind another window
These realities are exchanged;
Divorced as we are
From the unseen enemy.

Jackie Curry

Orion Slave Girl

With seaweed twist
And sensuous swirl
She takes the stage
Serpentine limbs
Dark drift of hair
Flowing
Aquamarine sheen on
Silk soft skin

They call her slave
Dancing girl
Whose burning eyes
And snarling lips
Hold us thrall
Captive;
Fierce dominatrix
Of our dreams

Ruth Berman

Nightingale Woman

My love has wings, slender, feathered things,
With grace in upswept curve and tapered tip,
Soft and sliding underneath the grip
Of my bewildered, alien hands. She sings:
Curving tunes that bind my mind in rings
Of turning sound, soft silver notes that rip
My heart, though they are gentle as the dip
And swirl of brown and russet on her wings.
It is impossible that we should fit
Body to body, desire to desire.
My lips touch hers. She sings afresh,
Voice rising like the double moon that lit
Us through her trees. She steps from her attire.
Her wings spread wide, then close about my flesh.

Ruth Berman

The Turning of the Inland Tide
(Kirk's childhood)

In Iowa, where no sea sounds,
Upon no sandy shore
A boy sat reading of the wine-dark sea.
Odysseus he was, and Gilgamesh,
Hornblower, Noah, Da Gama,
And John Paul Jones:
Drake's drum
Pounding
In the surges of his blood.

In Iowa, where no sea sounds,
Upon no sandy shore,
A boy sat reading till the sun went down,
And left his page a blank
That glimmered like the foam.
He raised his head.

One silver satellite
Flashed through the wine-dark sky.

Ian Duhig

At Quark's Bar, Deep Space Nine

My maker took your fascists' cartoon-Jew,
Scaled back its nose but gave me ears like clams
So I won't take abuse, old chap, from you
Cocksure from pornographic holograms.
Consider an off-camera position:
You called me Shylock when I brought your bill;
I've read outside the Rules of Acquisition
And never bought this worship of your Will -
The 'many-coloured life'* he gave each part?
Did that include his Jewish moneylender?
He makes the bar-bill read like Jean-Paul Sartre.
You're new, so I don't write you off, big spender,
But I keep tabs and bills and records straight.
Now pay. I'm not here just to educate.

*Samuel Johnson

TO BOLDLY GLOW;
poems of love and lust

Linda France

Star Trek Sestina

It is among the Klingons that love poetry
achieves its fullest flower
Lieutenant Worf

There isn't much I don't know about love.
It's a point of honour for a Klingon -
to go beyond the final frontier;
to be open and fearless, the Captain
and the crew of their starship passions.Space
is a place for loving: do it boldly.

Fall in love boldly so you'll write boldly.
You can't have one without the other.Love
is a white-hot black hole in outer space;
light is fast and lonely. Whisper Klingon
galactic sweet talk and, like our Captain,
you'll never fail to cross the frontier.

A lot's been said about that frontier,
a lot of jokes about going boldly.
But you've got to admit Kirk and Captain
Picard - neither of them went short on love.
We taught them all they knew of the Klingon
arts of desire, singing sonnets in space.

To write poems you need plenty of space.
Every line is a new frontier
of pain. And it's true, lovers *can* cling on,
anxious and craving. Just tell them boldly
how many moons you must orbit for love
of their phaser thighs. Show them who's Captain.

That's one of life's ironies our Captain
understands: the more you love, the less space
you have; not world's enough or time to love
forever; no cosmos, no frontier

far enough to hold it all. Compose boldly
in your own tongue. I'll read it in Klingon.

There's something about the sound of Klingon
that drives all sane beings wild; the Captain
included I must confess. *Go boldly,
Jean-Luc* is all I need to say. Then space
ripples between us and no frontier
remains. We're one on our planet of love.

I am the Captain of couplets in space.
Let me boldly erase this frontier,
my love, your clothes. Trust me, I'm a Klingon.

Deryn Rees-Jones

Lovesong to Captain James T. Kirk

Captain. I never thought we'd come to this,
but things being what they are, being adults,
stardate '94 it's best to make the best of it
and laugh. What's done is done. Perhaps
I'll start to call you Jim or Jamie, James....

No one was more shocked than me when I arrived
(the lady doth protest) to find
my bruised and rainy planet disappeared
and me, materialised and reconstructed
on board the Starship Enterprise, all 60s
with my laquered bee-hive and my thigh-high
skirt in blue, my Doc Marten's and my jeans
replaced by skin-tight boots
and scratchy blue-black nylons rippling
up my less-than-perfect calves. Sulu
looked worried. Spock cocked up one eyebrow
enigmatically, branding my existence
perfectly illogical. How nice, I thought. His ears.
Uhura smiled of course, and fiddled
with her hair. *O James.* Truth is
I loved you even as a child.....

O slick-black-panted wanderer holding
your belly in, your phaser gun
on stun, and eyes like Conference pears.
You're not my type but I undress
you, and we fuck
and I forgive your pancake make-up and mascara,
the darker shadows painted round your eyes.
The lava-lamp goes up and down. We're
a strange unison. Politically
Mismatched. Our mutual friend
The Doc takes notes. *Go easy Bones!*

Scotty is beaming and shouts *Energise*,
and all of a sudden you remind me
Of my dad, my brother and my mum,
my body rising like a shadow from the past
on top of you. As I press your arms behind your head
I drape my breasts so that you
brush my nipples gently with your lips almost
involuntarily as we boldly go. Come slowly, Captain,
and we do, with both our pairs of eyes tight closed.

Kitty Fitzgerald

I'm getting no response Captain

There was nothing plastic
about Uhura's thighs
not their size, not the way they
swayed from side to side.

Captain's Log: Stardate 2.2045.
Lost in the Absalom Belt.
Must do something about Uhura's replies

Not their sweet parting
or departure
or the way her boots
nipped in below the knee
seductively.

Captain's Log: Stardate 3.2045.
Somewhere near Alpha Fotora.
Must do something about Uhura's disguise.

When Scottie lost phaser power,
one crossed-leg manoeuvre
would get him out of orbit,
into a dream about the place
between her thighs

Captain's Log: Stardate 4.2045
Approaching the Leya System.
Must do something about Uhura's exercise.

If Chekov's voice trembled,
is it any wonder?
she energised the Enterprise,
science and sexuality melded
into that deep space.

Captain's Log; Stardate 5.2045.
Orbiting the Nimbaud Sun.
Must do something about Uhura's thighs.

Carol Coiffait

On Earth we Pon Farr when we can

Spock, you grim old Vulcan
I'm going to rip that skin-tight
suit right off, peel you to the bone.
I'll make you raise more than an eyebrow
when I dress you in more homely gear:
a tartan shirt perhaps and baggy
denims tucked into gumboots.

I want to see you stepping out
into the rain to slop your hogs
on a remote homestead
somewhere up in Maine.

I have arranged for surgery
on those great lugs of yours
so's you can wear a beat-up hat
in sun or snow and hail, until your cap
of laquered hair grows long enough
to curl around its brim.

And I'll tail you into town,
you in your old pick-up, me in mine,
on your monthly jaunt to market
to trade your surplus eggs and veg,
your bacon and prize hams.

I'll be in Data's Bar before you
to watch you join your farming pals.
You'll chew the fat about untimely
frosts, the price of feed and corn,
and raise a glass or three as you-all
reminisce about the times you had
with poor old Bones.

When you set out for home, it's pretty
late, past two o'clock, so you drive
fast but keep an eye out for Traffic
Cops. Jouncing down your own dirt-
track towards your comely wife
your long face cracks.

Aproned and floured to her elbows
she smiles and asks you how it goes.
You answer inappropriately, I fear....
'What is this thing called love
if it's not here?'
Then grab your Honey by her ample rear.

She screams: 'Your trousers, Dennis....'
Your face just splits from ear to ear.

footnote; the Pon Farr, or mating urge in Vulcans, occurs once every
seven years. It is a powerful biological upheaval that cannot be
resisted without risking death.

W.N. Herbert

Ode to Scotty

We kent ut wiz yir accent that
they couldna tak much mair o -
thae engines - foarmed somewhaur atween
Belfast and Ontario.

O Mister Scott, weel may ye talk
aboot WARP Factor Seven:
you tuke thi clash o Brigadoon -
transpoartit ut tae Heaven.

But still we luve ye tho ye werr
a Canuck in disguise:
tho Spock an Banes baith fanciet Kirk
you luved thi Enterprise.

Noo that we aa could undirstaund
fur ilka Scoatsman dotes
oan engines - see hoo Clydesiders
still bigg thir wee toy boats.,

An syne therr wiz yir pash fur booze
fae Argyle tae Arcturus;
ye ootdrank Klingons grecht an smaa -
anither trait no spurious.

We kent dilithium crystals werr
(tho in thir future foarm)
thi semm gems that ye find gin you
crack stanes aroond Cairngorm.

An whit a bony fechtir, eh?
Sae martial a revure,
while Kirk left you in oarbit fur
three-quaartirs o an oor

while he an Spock an Banes plunked aff
tae some furbidden planit
ye kent they werr oan lusty splores
but still ye birled lyk granite.

But maist o aa we luve ye coz
ye saved oor naishun's fiss:
ye nivir whinged aboot Englan but -
ye beat thum intae Space!

clash: local speech; *ilka*: each; *bigg*: build; *syne*: then; *gin*: if ;
revure: look of contempt; *plunked aff*: played truant; *splores*: jaunts;
birled: spun.

Jocelyn Boileau

Just trekking

Amid falling cotton seed
I glide
        ...on a glass lake
and with each rhythmic
paddle dip
I dream of being
cast adrift
        ...with Jean-Luc
on cosmic waters.

Eileen Jones

Take me to your ready room

Jean-Luc Picard, please let it be my fate
to count the stars reflected in your pate.
It's no surprise I've fallen hard for you;
you're in a different quadrant from your crew.

Will Riker, brave but not as sharp as most,
is not your thinking woman's piece of toast.
While Geordi's mind is crisply analytical,
there's no way he could get my warp core critical.
Nor could Data, though his bits are all correct
and he has by far the biggest intellect.
And Worf? I couldn't snuggle up in bed
to someone with a corrugated head.

As for the women, anyone can see
they yearn for you, Jean-Luc and just like me,
they hear that wistful timbre in your voice.
But look around you. Have you got a choice?

That stuck-up medic, Crusher? Surely not.
Who spawns a kid like Wesley should be shot.
Don't even think of making Troy your squeeze.
An interstellar social worker? Please!
And Guinan? Leave her to her Vulcan gin
and Klingon cocktails. You're not taken in
by seers in silly hats; you're too perceptive.
Besides, her name sounds like a contraceptive.*

Mon Caiptaine tout seul! It's me you seek:
your cup of Earl Grey tea, I'm hot and weak.
We're meant to be, Jean-Luc, it's futile to resist;
you might escape the Borg, mon cher, but I'll persist.
Oh beam me to your side! You have to know
I'm yours, Jean-Luc, if you'll just make it so.

*Gynon Alpha femidons: the Galactic prophylactic, tested by Klingons

Max Scratchmann

Resistance is Futile

She stands so taut and severe
in her Borg bondage gear
barking
'Resistance is futile'
although
I have no intention of resisting her

'Assimilate me! Assimilate me!'
I gasp, thrusting closer to the TV set,
but prime-time reality kicks in
just in time
and she quickly gains
blonde hair and mascara

Resistance is futile.............

Roseann Pannier-Taylor

The Creator

You were the great bird of the Galaxy
Who fell to earth to create dreams
For those of us who wanted to follow you
Into the stars boldly going
Through unchartered space.

You gave us something to depend on,
A hope for the future
With all of its possibilities
Of equality for all
Despite our supposed differences.

We shall miss you, Gene Roddenberry
And, we promise that your dreams will
Live long and prosper.

STAR TREK
the Haiku

Ruth Berman

6683 Hollywood Boulevard Haiku

Gilt star glitters in
sun on the sidewalk:
Gene's, from beyond Antares

Giovanni Malito

to boldly go...

and why not?--
when everything else
was possible
what's a split infinitive?

Jack Holt

S.T.: the Next Haiku

Precious green liquid
pooling upon alien soil.
Bones says: 'He's dead, Jim'

Sean Russell Friend

Haiku from a table in Ten Forward

Guinan is my friend:
I know by her knowing smile -
Her womb carries Time....

Haiku from Transporter Room Three

In the matter - stream,
we're alone in broken time,
half in waking dream....

Sharon Caseburg

Haiku for the Crystalline Entity

Luminous beauty
shimmers through the galaxy -
destruction and death

Hassan Masum

'To Boldly Go...'
Haiku Pentacycle

Ever outward bound,
Spirits sailing the seas of
Limitless space-time.

New worlds,new peoples...
Infinite diversity
instantiated.

In uncharted skies
We fight,we laugh,and we die
With honour and pride!

Seeking kindred souls,
Each new species reminds us:
We are not alone.

On infinite worlds,
The universe comes to life --
Oh, to see it all!

BEYOND THE FINAL FRONTIER
episodes as yet unwritten

Ian McMillan

The Lost Barnsley Episode
of which only Fragments Remain

In which Captain Kirk is seen, briefly,
before a silhouetted pithead

and Mr. Spock looks quizzical
beside a line of police vans.

Scotty says the engines won't take any more
so the soup is cold in the soup kitchen

and Bones looks quizzical
beside a line of pickets

with 1970's haircuts
even though it is the 1980's

and the crew of the Enterprise
have 1960's haircuts.

History comes down to this:
haircuts, quizzical looks,

someone saying that the engines
won't take any more

and then the engines slowly die.
William Shatner said of Barnsley,

during the filming,
'Some of these guys

have bigger bellies than me!
What are all these cops doing here?'

William Shatner missing the point,
at least briefly,

is the plot of most Star Trek episodes
is the plot of most of the Eighties.

Valerie Laws

Don't Put your Daughter into Space, Mrs Kirk

What happens to old spacewomen?
Or even slightly middle aged?
In the future of equal opportunities, no job
is closed to women (save Captain).
They rocket up, Chief This, Commander That,
while barely in their twenties; heads,
we presume, full of micro-circuits, they sway
the shining corridors of starships,
in skin-tight catsuits

But while the men, of varying handsomeness,
spread, go grey, and dare
to baldly go where no woman has before
(towards an old age pension)
they disappear. Sent home perhaps to breed
their brains and beauty into future crews,
or jettisoned in hyper-space, like garbage.
Perhaps beamed down to some obscure planet,
to join a crowd of ageing women
with degrees in astrophysics
discovering the joy of leaving their mascara off.

It must be hard to save the ship from aliens,
all the while waiting for the signal
to drop out of active service,
being no longer quite so ornamental.
Does a specially assigned ship's officer scan
the female personnel, alert
for wrinkles or a sagging bum?
Do they go quietly, unasked, but warned by instinct
like elephants did (when there were elephants):
or screaming, bundled out the airlock
while the camera's elsewhere?

It will remain a mystery, like Dr. Who's toilet.
But better to kill them, Captain. Or else one day,
an angry maenad-horde of beautiful old women
will storm your bridge, knowing exactly where
to pull your plug out.

Alan Boag

Boldly.

We've searched the galaxy bit by bit
For infinitives to boldly split.

Where none had boldly gone before
The Prime Directive we'd ignore.

We've boldly made the brave decision
To boldly go on one last mission;

It's Scotty's final claim to fame,
The mighty Warp Nine zimmer frame.

Bob Wakulich

Not On This Voyage

' I sense pain, ' said Troi, edging forward
in her chair. ' Maybe Doctor Crusher
can give you a shot.'
I shook my head.
' Perhaps you are hungry,' said Data.
' We have a variety
of foodstuffs available.'
' No, ' I said.
' We can't help you
if you won't tell us
what's wrong,' said Riker.
' We have the finest technology
and the best minds of the Federation
at our disposal,' said Picard. ' Surely
they can be of assistance here.'
' I have to go to the bathroom,' I said.
Picard rubbed his hands together.
' Do we have any bathrooms ? '
' A true warrior doesn't go to the bathroom,'
said Worf.
' I have read about bathrooms,' said Data.
' I sense dismay,' said Troi.

The Love-Song of Zefrem Cochran
(U.N.S.S. Bonaventure, Tau Ceti, May 2061)

The shadow of the bird has marked the wall,
blackened my face, drawn the eyes of the
stranger ever closer, and I am afraid, for the
dark is behind and the red wave of evening is
crashing down. The darkness has come to
claim the turning away; the turning half of all
I am, and ever will be: this blue O the world
stage from which we fly, and dip a toe in star-
light. The roar of flight; the rush of distance
come, dashing over the edge of time. The face
of God is masked in shame. We out-stride our
Maker, and have arrived, never the same again.

Our craft has found your beauty. A sperm to
ovum. The opiate aired curve we ride to. Invade
its virgin mist, and twist to land. There are met
by a white star's rising and a dewed green that
wets bare feet. As we alight - the smaller step is
hers. Mine is a greater leap that takes me nowhere.
There is a moon under which something pulls
like a spider's web or the slackened strings of
the Aolean harp - like plain-song in empty space.
The first night we are Adam and Eve, and with
the first light I awake to find a monster, or wiser
being, has taken the guts of my sleeping friend.
I recall her last words; 'This is going to be fun...'
and cast what I loved into our quantam fire.

The rain outside is making the grass greener, and the pale cheeks of remembered friends a delusion, when choosing raindrops, or tears, as the most eloquent metaphor for grief. She is our first dead: the queen and mother of this new world; the un-leven saviour of our cynical faith. Alone again, the Vitruvian man does somersaults like a harlequin; his mad hands and feet grasping at their full extent, the limits, the very edge. So she went into Heaven - that is all we comprehend; the figures do not add up; the theories are always flawed and God still laughs behind the proscenium arch.

Steve Sneyd

Three Generations After Enterprise Contact

at feet
of double god
are laid their young to let
stone incarnation ears sky spires
choose eat

priests prove
this gift of blood
brings ever nearer back
across starwheel divine ship will
end pain

toil is
temporary
burden death too will die
when proved faith works deserve second
coming

John Light

Enterprising English

Our mission is to boldly go,
to carelessly split infinitives
no-one has split before.
To countless worlds we'll warp the words
scattering various parts of speech
' wider still and wider,'
and so bestow on aliens
the blessed unity of English
(infinitives apart),
to willingly teach their grammars
to metaphorically suck eggs
till they understand us.

Alison Chisholm

Close Encounter

CAPTAIN'S LOG....

For days now we have been orbiting
a cloud of unidentified matter.
The crew are baffled; the computer cannot probe
the mass of data stored within.
We have put up our shields
and engaged maximum warp -
but we cannot escape the tractor beam
that drags us back.

From its interior the cloud exudes
a kind of music. All who recognise it
make report of different frequencies, as if
each hears a song unique to each,
sways to a unique rhythm.

Even the Betazoid cannot decipher
nuances of meaning issuing
from the cloud's depths. Only
when its mists thin, she reads a hint
of its message - enough to know
it is trying to communicate.

The delay is causing problems. We are aiming
to get back on course - and yet
my officers are finding it difficult to concentrate,
obsessed with learning all about the cloud.

CAPTAIN'S LOG SUPPLEMENTAL....

The whole ship's company is now engaged
in analysing the amorphous mass. At least
we have a designation for it now.
It's called a poem.

U.A. Fanthorpe

Alien in Residence

(for Tony Childs and Katherine Fanthorpe,
who helped me to boldly go)

It had come to be a resident, it said.
It arrived compatibly. We had just
Re-vitalised the primary sensors,
When it beamed up in the observation lounge,
Equipped with a name, a hologram, a protocol.
Utterly unfamiliar. Of course, we ran
A security diagnostic. It seemed OK.
Not a war-lord, certainly. Hadn't
a click of Klingon. Ears of
Humanoid texture, forehead no more corrugated
Than is commensurate with prolonged thought.
The Captain saw it as a malfunction
From the start. *Energy disruption field,*
He muttered. Also *Quantum singularity.*
Try another sensor reading. Sir! We snapped to it;
But all our serializations were identical.

It spoke our tongue. Shook hands with the Captain
(A social gaffe) and kissed Uhura (indelicate).
Produced documentation. Spoke of Arts,
And a Council (not known to our Federation),
Uttered in a pronounced anti-graviton layer.
Produced books (how did Galactic customs let them
                                            through?)
Signed them; tried to sell them.

A hostile simulation programme (Doc's diagnosis)
It can't stay here, on the final frontier,
using up words (and it's true,
It used a whole gravometric singularity
Of glossary, words like rhythm, rap, metaphor,
Irony, image, Shakespeare, none of which
We understood). *Energy relays are corroded*,
Says the engineer. *Affirmative*, says Captain.
All hands to psyonic resonators.
                                    So we vaporised it,
Making ourselves safe to experience
Civilisation as we know it,

The Star Trek Poets

Kevin Bailey:
poet, founder/editor of Haiku Quarterly Magazine since
1990. Haiku anthology and new poetry collection
(University of Salzburg) due out this year. Also an
astronomer, has 21" telescope and has lent pencils to
Patrick Moore. Fan of ST since 1969.

David Bateman:
first poetry collection Curse of the Killer Hedge (IRON
Press, 96), next one The Sweetness of Nightingales due
out soon. Performs widely, currently writing a history of
Liverpool poety for Headland Press. shamelessly enjoyed
Blake's 7.

Ruth Berman:
lives in Minneapolis, USA, and has had many poems and
stories published in SF magazines and anthologies eg
Asimov's, Weird Tales, Analog.

Alan Boag:
is a fifty something Housing Manager living in Scotland,
who discovered Star Trek as a student in the sixties and
has been a fan ever since, preferring the original series
to its imitators.

Joyce Boileau:
from Wales, is a freelance writer living in Winnipeg,
Manitoba; many poems and articles published including a
chapbook, Venus Rising, with her writer's group.

Cathy Bolton:
lives in Manchester and works for Commonword Community
publishers. Poems widely published, most recently in Rialto
and Brando's Hat. Currently writing a novel.

Kevin Cadwallender:
lives in Sunderland, music journalist, has been poet in residence for Great North Forest, Poet in the Co-op in Cumbria. Many pamphlets published; first poetry collection, Public (IRON Press, 2000)

Sharon Caseburg:
poet and Star Trek fan living in central Canada. Her works have appeared in journals and anthologies. She is an MA in English Literature.

Cy Chaney:
this is his first published poem, he knows it won't be his last. He says his stuff is intense, extreme, slipstream, in one word - potent. Lives in Kirby, Notts.

Debjani Chatterjee:
Indian-born poet, editor and children's writer. Lives in Sheffield. Recent books include Albino Gecko (Univ.of Salzburg) and The Redbeck Anthology of British South Asian Poetry (Redbeck Press). Reviews Editor of Writing in Education.

Alison Chisholm:
teaches creative writing on Merseyside, is poetry consultant for BBC Radio Merseyside. Has had seven poetry collections published, latest being Daring the Slipstream (Headland,97). Has written books on creative writing.

G.O.Clark:
works in a university library in Davis, California; long time Star Trek and Grateful Dead fan but neither Deadhead or Trekkie; poetry published in Star* Line (also reviews) Asimov's Outer Darkness magazines; describes life as pretty ho hum.

Mandy Coe:

lives in Liverpool, Planet Earth, where she writes poetry
for adults and children. Her first collection for adults
published Spring 2000.

Carol Coiffait:

from East Yorkshire; regular reader at Hull Lit Fest, published in Acumen, Fatchance, Proof and children's anthologies (Scholastic, Nelson & Longman). Has written for art
installation (HLF99), dance, drama and video.

Cardinal Cox:

current chairbadger (sic) of Peterborough SF Club; articles, reviews, stories and poems publisihed in The
Brobignagian Times, Dark Fantasy Newsletter et al. Twice
runner up in Poet Laureate of Peterborough competition

Jackie Curry:

works as a School Health Adviser in Warwickshire. A Star
Trek fan since the beginning, she is now passionate about
DS9. Poetry and short story published in zines of Andrew
Robinson fan club.

Keith Allen Daniels:

chemist by training, poet, editor and publisher with poems
in Analog SF, Asimov's Science Fiction, Weird Tales and
other strange places. Lives in California, enjoys making
funny voices, aspires to play guitar.

Ian Duhig:

has taught creative writing all over the globe, won the
National Poetry competition in 87, and lives in Leeds.
Three acclaimed collections: The Bradford Count, chosen
for Poetry Soc's New Generation List; The Mersey Goldfish,
shortlisted for TS Eliot prize, and Nominies, Sunday Times
Poetry Book of the Year in 98.

U.A. Fanthorpe:

after Oxford taught for sixteen years before becoming a
middle-aged drop-out, working as a clerk/receptionist at
a Bristol neurological hospital. Seven collections of poetry,
and Selected Poems (King Penguin, 86) Fellow of Royal
Society of Literature and Poet in Residence at various
places. Lives in Gloucestershire.

Kitty Fitzgerald:
Irish-born, best known as a novelist and playwright. IRON
Press published a joint collection of poetry, For Crying Out
Loud, (with Valerie Laws) in 1994. Her latest novel,
Snapdragons, was published Oct 99 by Brandon. Fell for
Captain Kirk's pecs in the 60s

Linda France:
Hexham, Northumberland based poet, currently writer in
residence at Mowbray Park, Sunderland. Three collections
published by Bloodaxe books, Red, The Gentleness of the
Very Tall and Storyville. New collection due 2001. Editor
of Sixty Women Poets (Bloodaxe).

Sean Russell Friend:
best known for gothic comedy novels, including Vampyre
Jazz; TV scriptwriter for Eastenders, Ballykissangel,
Casualty; has acted in TV programmes such as Ultraviolet
and The Last Train

Desmond Graham:
lecturer in English at Universityof Newcastle upon Tyne;
editor and biographer of Keith Douglas; and editor of
anthology, Poetry of the Second World War (Pimlico).
He has had three collections of poetry published, The
Marching Bands, The Lie of Horizons, and Not Falling
(seren, 99)

Scott E Green:
widely published sf poet, Manchester(USA) based, twice
moninated for Rhysling; market news editor of STAR*LINE,
his poetry chapbook, Private Worlds is online by
Ebooksonthe.net. Reference book on genre poetry published by Greenwood, 89.

W N Herbert:
Dundee-born, Oxford DPhil, lives Newcastle, teaches cre-
ative writing at Lancaster University. Dreams of a trans-
Pennine transporter. Writes in English and Scots. Several
collections published by Bloodaxe, the lates being The
Laurelude (98)

Jack Holt:
is an Arizona native, who attended college at MIT, where the only time you saw everyone in the dorm at once was when SF was on. His Nerdly Jaikus website is a collection of sci-fi haikus.

Eileen Jones:
lives in Wylam, Northumberland;has written for nearest and dearest for many years;recently had poems published in The Red Herring (Northern Poetry Library) and read at the Blue Room, Newcastle upon Tyne.

Lindsay Kelly:
lives on the Sussex coast with husband and two cats, works as PA for firm of financial advisers and has been a Star Trek fan since childhood.

Deborah P. Kolodji:
uses her information technology career in California to finance a poetry habit; recent work published in Star*Line, Dreams & Nightmares, and Orphic Chronicle.

John Light:
lives in Berwick upon Tweed, is the author of three sci fi novels, including The Lords of Hate, (Photon Press, 97), many short stories, poems and drawings, nine books for children, and has four poetry collections published

Giovanni Malito:
is a Canadian of italian origin, living in Ireland where he lectures in Chemistry. He publishes The Brobdingnagian Times; has poetry published in Orbis, The Yellow Crane, Poetry Motel et al.

Joy H Mann:
English-born, runs a junkstore in Ontario, Canada; Leacock Award for Poetry 97. Work in many magazines including Cosmic Unicorn, On Spec, Jackhammer. Collection published in Alien Songs, 1997*, Roswell, New Mexico Anthology.

Hassan Masum:
PhD student living in Ottawa, Canada, who has worked as a scientist, programmer and engineer. He likes problem-solving, and is proud to be part of humanity's slow ascent.

Ian McMillan:
much published poet and performer, frequent broadcaster on BBC Radio 4, Ian is Barnsley Football Club poet in residence and favours William Shatner rather than DeForest Kelly in the matter of girth.

Shirley Meech:
retired secretary and contracts administrator in Los Angeles; Star Trek fan since the very first episode. Work published in T-Negative and Star Trek - the New Voyages (Bantam story anthology)

Mike Morgan:
finance assistant for the NHS in Stoke on Trent, artist and illustrator, has published stories, reviews, articles on Doctor Who for Beccon publications and British Mensa fanzine Ice Hot Doctor.

Roseann Pannier-Taylor:
an American living in England since marriage in 94, hopes always to remain an ardent Star Trek fan, works part-time hoping to make a living from writing and poetry.

Karen R Porter:
resides in the haunted pinelands of New Jersey in a ramshackle abode full of critters; claims her dreams are strange and she scans the skies with hope.

Sheenagh Pugh:
lives in Cardiff, Wales, has had nine collections of poems published by Seren, the lates being Stonelight (Seren 99). She is a Senior Lecturer in Creative Writing at University of Glamorgan. Poem sequence Fanfic published online.

Deryn Rees-Jones:
lives in Liverpool. She was given an Eric Gregory Award by the Society of Authors and had a play, The Nightmare, performed in London in 1994. Poetry collectons published by Seren, the lates being Sighs Round A Dead Body.

Max Scratchmann:
lives in the Orkney Islands; illustrator, poet, multi-media artist; his London solo show, Painting Fairies, was a fusion of art and poetry, thirteen pieces of 3-D art linking together to illustrate a verse text.

Patrick Snape:
was joint winner of Gizza Poem, a national poetry competition judged by Alan Bleasdale and Jimmy McGovern, and runner up in another one he's forgotten the name of. Lives in Newcastle upon Tyne.

Steve Sneyd:
lives in Huddersfield, West Yorks. Many science fiction poems published in magazines and broadcast on Radio 4 in 96; has read at many festivals and SF conventions. Collection published in In Coils of Earthen Hold (Salzburg University Press). Won Peterson trophy in poetry slam at Small Press Festival in 96.

Subhadassi:
is a poet living in Newcastle upon Tyne. His work has appeared in magazines, on radio, over the Metro and on Tyne Tees TV, and a pamphlet, Sublunary Voodoo (Mudfog, 98). Currently working on a first collection.

Stephen Wade:
lectures in English at University of Huddersfield; reviews for magazines including Agenda, Acumen. Three poetry collections. latest being on Adult Education (Stone Creek, 98). Also writes fiction.

Bob Wakulich:
teaches at College of the Rockies in British Colombia, Canada; has MFA in Creative Writing from University of BC. Fiction, poetry and non-fiction published in various magazines and anthologies eg Paris/Atlantic, Sub Terrain, and numerous websites.

Rodney Wood:
works in Guildford for a quango; has published over a hundred poems in various magazines with more to come.

✓✓✓✓✓✓✓✓

Valerie Laws is an associate editor of IRON Press, and a prize-winning poet, published in many magazines and anthologies and a joint collection (with Kitty Fitzgerald), For Crying Out Loud (IRON). She is a graduate in English and in Maths, currently doing an MA at the University of Northumbria